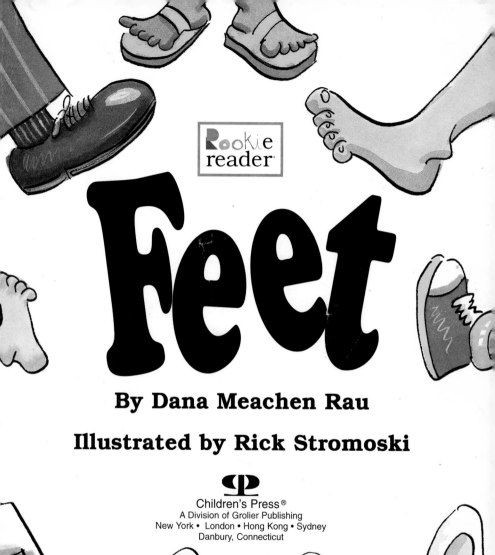

Feet

By Dana Meachen Rau

Illustrated by Rick Stromoski

Children's Press®
A Division of Grolier Publishing
New York • London • Hong Kong • Sydney
Danbury, Connecticut

For Charlie
—D.M.R.

For Jaqie and Molly Stromoski
—R.S.

Reading Consultants
Linda Cornwell
Coordinator of School Quality and Professional Improvement
(Indiana State Teachers Association)

Katharine A. Kane
Education Consultant
(Retired, San Diego County Office of Education
and San Diego State University)

Visit Children's Press® on the Internet at:
http://publishing.grolier.com

Library of Congress Cataloging-in-Publication Data
Rau, Dana Meachen.
    Feet / by Dana Meachen Rau; illustrated by Rick Stromoski.
      p. cm. — (Rookie reader)
    Summary: Brief rhyming text describes children at camp who use their feet to do a variety of things, from kicking a soccer ball to rollerblading.
    ISBN 0-516-22008-X (lib.bdg.)   0-516-27042-7 (pbk.)
    1. Foot Juvenile literature. 2. Camping Juvenile literature. [1. Foot. 2. Camps.]
I. Stromoski, Rick, ill. II. Title. III. Series.
QM549.R38 2000
612'.98—dc21
                                           99-30169
                                       CIP

GROLIER
PUBLISHING 1 2 3 4 5 6 7 8 9 10 R 09 08 07 06 05 04 03 02 01 00

3

Feet.

Feet can ride.

Feet can kick.

Feet can glide.

11

Feet are quick.

13

Feet can hike.

Feet can run.

17

Feet can bike.

Feet have fun!

21

Feet.

Word List (12 words)

are	have
bike	hike
can	kick
feet	quick
fun	ride
glide	run

About the Author

Dana Meachen Rau is the author of many books for children, including historical fiction, storybooks, biographies, and early readers. She has written *A Box Can Be Many Things*, *Purple Is Best*, *Circle City*, and *Bob's Vacation* (which she also illustrated) in the Rookie Reader series. Dana also works as a children's book editor and lives with her husband, Chris, and son, Charlie (who just discovered his feet), in Farmington, Connecticut.

About the Illustrator

Rick Stromoski is an award-winning humorous illustrator whose work has appeared in magazines, newspapers, children's books, advertising, and network television. He lives in Suffield, Connecticut, with his wife, Danna, and five-year-old daughter, Molly.

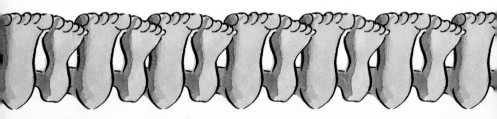